rockschool®

LET'S ROCK

START PLAYING NOW!

BASS

www.rslawards.com

rockschool

ACKNOWLEDGEMENTS

Published by Rockschool Ltd. © 2013
Catalogue Number RSK121302
ISBN: 978-1-908920-38-6
Revision 1 | 7 March 2014

AUDIO

Recorded, mixed and mastered at Langlei Studios by Duncan Jordan
Producer: James Uings

MUSICIANS

Stuart Clayton, Neel Dhorajiwala, Noam Lederman, Jon Musgrave, Charlie Griffiths

PUBLISHING

Publishing Manager: James Uings
Editorial Manager: Stephen Lawson
Written by Stuart Clayton
Music engraving by Simon Troup and Jennie Troup of Digital Music Art
Logo design by Bryn Reynolds
Proofing: Becky Baldwin and Simon Bradley

SYLLABUS

Syllabus Director: Jeremy Ward
Instrumental specialists: Stuart Clayton, Noam Lederman and James Uings

PRINTING

Printed and bound in the United Kingdom by Caligraving Ltd

PHOTOGRAPHY

Photographer: Adam Gasson
Bassist: Becky Baldwin

DISTRIBUTION

Exclusive Distributors: Music Sales Ltd

CONTACTING ROCKSCHOOL

www.rslawards.com
Telephone: +44 (0)845 460 4747
Email: *info@rslawards.com*

Awarding the
Contemporary Arts

CONTENTS

WELCOME

Welcome to Let's Rock Bass!

This book will guide you through the basics of rock and pop bass playing. It has been designed to build your skills and knowledge as you work your way through the lessons. The book is split into three parts: Getting Started, Lessons and Pieces.

GETTING STARTED

The first section of the book contains all the information you will need before you begin your first lesson. This includes a guide to how your instrument works, an introduction to reading music and a walkthrough of all the basic techniques used in the book.

LESSONS

The lessons are split into styles of music and there are two parts for each style. You will practise musical examples which build up to a final example taken from a piece later in the book. There is

also space for teacher feedback at the end of every lesson.

PIECES

Once you have worked your way through the lessons you will be ready to practise and perform your first full pieces of music. There is one for every style of music covered in the lessons.

There are also three extra pieces which can be played on your own or as part of a band. The other band parts can be found in *Let's Rock Guitar* and *Let's Rock Drums* and the full band score is part of your downloadable package.

AUDIO

Every musical example and piece in *Let's Rock Bass* has two audio tracks that can be downloaded from the Rockschool website. The first is a full track that includes the bass part along with a full band.

The other is a backing track with the bass taken off so you can play along with the band.

DOWNLOAD

The downloadable content for this book can be downloaded from RSL directly at the following URL:

www.rslawards.com/downloads

When downloading files you will need to input this code when prompted: KGPFNSDMU9

The audio files are supplied in MP3 format, the most widely compatible audio format in common usage – MP3s will likely be familiar to anyone with a computer, iPod, smartphone or similar device. Once downloaded you will be able to play them on any compatible device; we hope that you find this extra versatility useful.

GETTING STARTED
INTRODUCTION

This section of *Let's Rock Bass* contains all the information you will need before you begin your first lesson. Over the next few pages you will find a guide to how your instrument works, all the techniques that are used throughout the book and an introduction to reading music.

THE BASS
A QUICK GUIDE
All you need to know about this amazing instrument

BASS GUITAR & AMPLIFIER

If you want to play bass you should first plug it in to an amplifier (amp). You could play the bass 'unplugged', but it would be too quiet to hear properly. Here are all the parts of the bass and amp that you need to know about…

PICKUPS
The pickups have magnets inside that sense the strings' vibrations. These smart devices then turn the vibrations into a signal that can be amplified (made loud) by an amplifier (or amp).

FRET BOARD
This is the area on the front of the neck where you place your fingertips.

VOLUME CONTROL
Turn this clockwise (from 0 to 10) to increase the volume of your bass.

BRIDGE
The strings are fixed at the body end of the bass by the bridge.

TONE CONTROL
Turn this clockwise (from 0 to 10) to increase the brightness of your bass's sound.

JACK PLUG
Plug a cable in here then plug the other end into your amp.

STRINGS

The bass's sound starts here. When you pluck a string it vibrates, making a note. How high or low the note sounds (its pitch) depends on where you press down on the string.

TUNING PEGS

Turn these to get your strings in tune. The best way to tune your bass is with an electronic tuner, or if you don't have one of these you could ask your teacher for some help.

FRETS

Frets divide the strings into separate notes.

FRET MARKERS

You can use the fret markers to quickly work out which fret is which. The following frets are usually marked: 3rd, 5th, 7th, 9th, 12th, 15th, 17th, 19th and 21st.

DID YOU KNOW

NECK

The strings are stretched across the length of the neck, which is shaped so you can place your fingers and thumb around it to play notes.

STRAP PINS

Attach a strap to these and you will be able to stand up while playing your bass.

The first bass guitar was invented by a man called Leo Fender. It went on sale in 1951 – over 60 years ago! – and was called the Fender Precision because, unlike the upright bass, the Precision (or P-Bass) had frets so bassists would know *precisely* where to place their fingers to play each note. The P-Bass was such a success that it is still on sale today and most other basses are based on its design.

CABLE Carries a signal from your bass's pickups to your amp.

AMPLIFIER

This makes your bass sound much louder than when it's unplugged. It has four basic controls: volume, bass, middle and treble. Volume makes the sound louder. The bass control makes the sound fuller and warmer. Treble is the opposite: it makes your bass sound light and sparkly. Middle is between bass and treble.

PLAYING THE BASS

You'll need to master these basic techniques to play the songs and examples in this book...

SITTING WITH YOUR BASS

2
Wrap your left hand around the neck of your bass and use your right hand to pull the body of the bass towards your body.

1
Sit in your chair with your feet shoulder width apart and pointing forward. Your shoulders should be relaxed but not slouching forward and your back straight.

3
The bass should sit straight up against your ribcage. Place the fingers of your right hand over the strings with your thumb resting on the string closest to your face. Your bass should rest on your right leg at a slight angle to your stomach. Face forward and keep your head up and shoulders back for good posture.

PLAYING WITH FINGERS

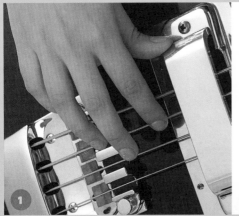

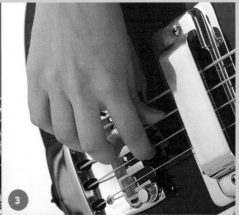

1 Place your thumb on top of the pickup cover. This is called anchoring because, like a ship's anchor, your thumb holds your hand in a steady position from which you will be able to pick the strings. Your fingers should point down across the strings.

2 Let's start by playing the E string – the thickest string on your bass. Use the pad, not the nail, of your first (pointing) finger to pluck the string. Try to move your finger just beyond the string (i.e. towards your thumb).

3 When playing the other strings you should take your thumb from the pickup cover and move it so it is sitting on the string next to the one you are playing. For example, if you are playing the D string your thumb should be anchored on the A string.

PLAYING WITH A PICK

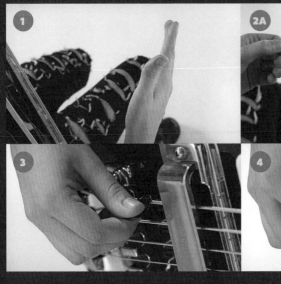
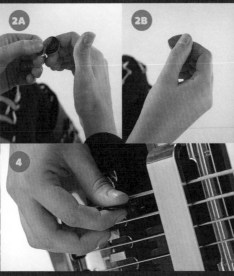

1 Some bassists prefer to play with a pick (also known as a plectrum). Here's how to do it… Take your right hand and turn it so your thumb is pointing upwards,

2 Keeping your thumb pointing straight up, curl your fingers back (2a) then (with your left hand) place the pick on top in the position shown and clamp your

Don't squeeze your fingers too much; your hand should be relaxed.

3 With your right forearm resting lightly on the body of your bass, hold the pick over the bottom (fattest) string. The tip of the pick should be just above the string. Hold the pick firmly between your thumb and index finger but keep your hand relaxed.

4 Move your wrist in a downward motion so that the tip of the pick strikes the string. Try to keep the movement as small as possible so that the pick goes only a few millimetres past the string. This means you will be able to move the pick quickly back to the starting position, ready to play

PLAYING NOTES

1 Wrap your left hand around the far end of the fretboard and place your thumb in the middle of the back of the neck. Everyone's hands are different, so don't worry if your thumb doesn't line up exactly as shown in the photo. Just make sure that the top – not the base – of your thumb is pressed against the neck and that your thumb doesn't go over the top of the neck.

2 Press your third (ring) finger on the 3rd fret of the E string while pressing on the back of the neck with your thumb. Your finger should be close to but not on top of the fret. You will find this uncomfortable at first but don't worry, you will soon build up strength and the discomfort will pass.

3 Bring your elbow forward, away from your body, so your wrist moves closer to the neck. This will raise your fingers so only your fingertips touch the strings.

4 Strike the string. You have just played your first note, a G!

HANDY HINT

In this book we will often refer to the left hand as the fretting hand, because it 'frets' the notes of the guitar. The right hand is known as the picking hand. Left-handed players should reverse this.

ONE FINGER PER FRET

As you play through the lessons and pieces in this book you should use what's called the one-finger-per-fret method. This means using your first finger to play the 1st fret, your second to play the 2nd and so on, as shown in the photo above. Notice how each finger is placed close to but not on top of each fret. This method means you can keep your hand more or less in one position and not have to move it around every time you need to play a different note.

HOW TO READ MUSIC

You'll be reading music in no time with this guide!

TAB

TAB is a very popular type of notation for bassists because you don't have to learn to read music before using it. TAB shows you what notes to play by placing numbers on top of four lines that represent the strings on the bass. The numbers refer to frets and tell you where to place your fingers on each string. But TAB doesn't show you when to play the notes nor how long each note should last. All of this information can be found on the musical stave...

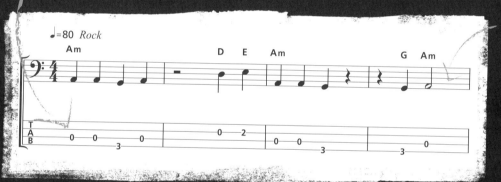

THE STAVE

The stave appears above the TAB and contains information on what notes to play, when to play them and how long to play them for. The stave consists of five lines. Notes can be placed on any of these lines or any space between the lines.

TEMPO, BARLINES & TIME SIGNATURES

Music is divided into groups of beats called bars. Vertical lines on the stave called barlines show where each bar begins and ends. The symbol with one number on top of another is the time signature. The top number tells you how many beats there are in each bar, while the bottom tells you what kind of beats they are. The time signature below shows there are four quarter notes in each bar, or 4/4 for short. You will learn about quarter notes in your first lesson. The tempo tells you how fast the song is, measured in beats-per-minute.

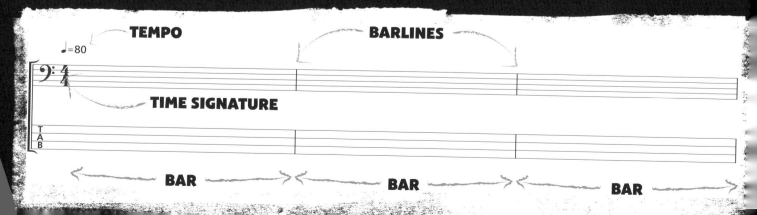

THE CLEF

This is the bass clef. It tells you which note each line and space of the stave represents. There are lots of different kinds of clefs which place the notes on different lines and spaces, but the bass clef is the only one you need to know for bass playing.

THE NOTES

The notes that fall on the lines of the stave can be remembered by the phrase 'Good Boys Deserve Fun Always'. The spaces between the lines can be remembered by 'All Cows Eat Grass'. You can, of course, make up your own phrases!

| G | B | D | F | A | A | C | E | G |
| Good | Boys | Deserve | Fun | Always | All | Cows | Eat | Grass |

RHYTHM

The rhythms in musical notation are described on the stave by different note heads and stems. These tell you where in the music each note should be played and how long it should be played for. The lessons that follow later in this book will cover different notes and rhythms.

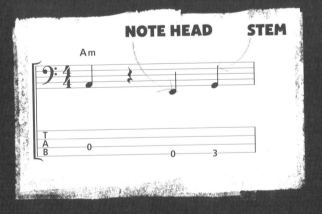

NOTE HEAD   STEM

DID YOU KNOW?

Music notation was first used in the Middle East over 3,000 years ago! Instructions for the words and melody of an ancient hymn were discovered in Syria on a clay tablet from around 1400 BC. People in those days used a stylus to carve symbols in wet clay. Once the clay was dry you couldn't make any changes – this was 3,000 years before electronic tablets!

NOTE VALUES

To help you remember the value of each note and rest you will come across in your lessons, we have included the diagrams below. These show the value of each note and rest relative to the others. So, for example, you can see that one whole note is the same length (or value) as four quarter notes…

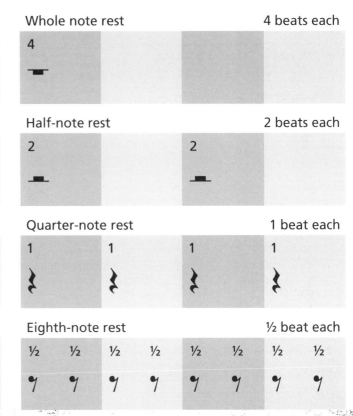

NOTE VALUES

Whole note		4 beats each

Half-note		2 beats each

Quarter-note		1 beat each

Eighth-note		½ beat each

REST VALUES

Whole note rest		4 beats each

Half-note rest		2 beats each

Quarter-note rest		1 beat each

Eighth-note rest		½ beat each

My Notes

LESSONS
INTRODUCTION

Now you understand how your instrument works and know how to read music and TAB, it's time for your first music lessons! These are split into different styles of music, with two parts for every style. You will practise short musical examples which build up to a final example at the end of each lesson, which is taken from a piece later in the book.

ROCK PART 1

In your first lesson you will learn two notes and play basslines using a quarter-note rhythm

DID YOU KNOW?

Flea is the bass player for the Red Hot Chili Peppers. He was influenced by funkbassplayers as well as rock and punk ones, so his style of music is known as funk rock.

WHAT YOU WILL LEARN
☑ Two notes: E and C
☑ Quarter-note rhythms
☑ Root notes

Rock is an interesting style of music for bass players because it offers lots of different ways to play the bass. In this style of music it is common to play with a pick (or plectrum) instead of the fingers. But don't worry, either method will work fine. Most rock bands have a singer, one or two guitars, bass and drums. AC/DC, Led Zeppelin and The Rolling Stones are some of the most famous rock groups. The bass is important in rock because it provides a solid backing for the other instruments and makes powerful rhythms with the drums.

CHORDS & ROOT NOTES

Many basslines in rock follow the chords and are based on root notes. Chords are made up of two or more notes and are usually played by guitars rather than bass. The root note is the most important note because the chord is named after it (e.g. the root of the E major chord is E).

Don't forget that audio is available for all the musical examples and pieces in this book. Full details on how to access the full band mixes and backing tracks can be found on page 4.

Example 1 — PLAYING QUARTER NOTES

Quarter notes last for one beat each. There are usually four beats and, therefore, four quarter notes in a bar, as in this example. Tap your foot or count along to the pulse (shown as '1 2 3 4' below) to help you play the notes at the right time.

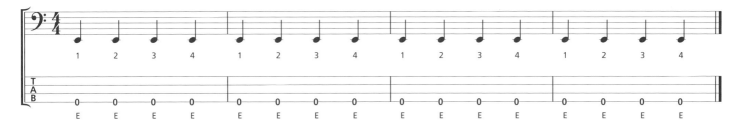

Example 2 — ACCENTING THE STRONG BEAT OF THE BAR

The first beat of every bar is the strongest and sounds slightly louder than the others. In this example you will play four quarter notes in each bar again, but this time play the first note of each bar slightly stronger than the others.

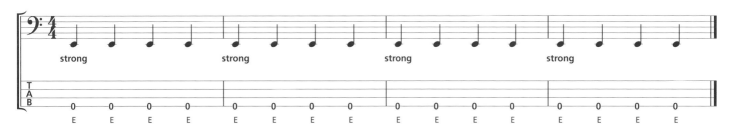

Example 3 — BASSLINE USING E & C NOTES

In this example you will use a new note: C. This note is found at the 3rd fret of the A string. Try to avoid fretbuzz when playing this example. Fretbuzz is an unwanted buzzing noise that happens when your fretting finger is too close to the fretwire. Tap your foot or count along to the pulse to help you play each note in time. The count you should use is shown below.

Teacher's Notes

Teacher's Rating

ROCK PART 2

In your second rock lesson you will be introduced to two new notes and the quarter-note rest

There are two ways to mute the strings. The first is with your picking hand...

...and the other is with your fretting hand. Rest your fingers gently on the strings

WHAT YOU WILL LEARN
☑ Two new notes: G and A
☑ Quarter-note rests

Part 1 of your rock lesson introduced the E note on the E string and quarter notes, which last for one beat each. In Part 2 you will learn about rests, which are the silent parts of music where you don't play anything. The first rest you will learn is a quarter-note rest, meaning this rest lasts for the same amount of time as a quarter note. When you see a rest in the music make sure you stop your bass from sounding by resting your fingers gently on the strings. This technique is called muting because you mute any notes from ringing on. By the end of this lesson you should be ready to tackle four bars of the piece 'Inferno' on page 42.

| Example 1 | **BASSLINE USING QUARTER-NOTE RESTS** |

This example has rests on the second and fourth beats of each bar. Don't let the notes from beats 1 and 3 ring through these beats. You can do this by placing both your hands lightly on the strings during the rests.

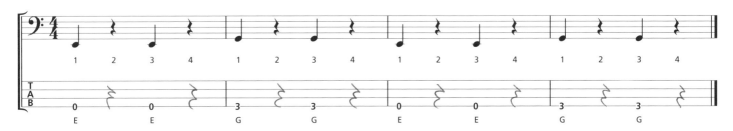

Example 2 — BASSLINE USING THREE NOTES

This exercise is another chance to play the C note which we learned in the last lesson, and features rests on beat 2 of each bar. Remember to keep your fretting finger close to but not on top of the fretwire to avoid fretbuzz.

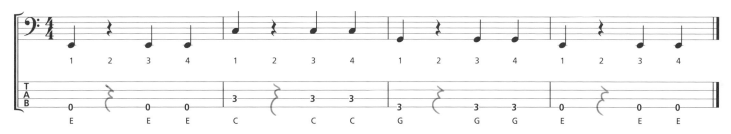

Example 3 — BASSLINE USING THREE NOTES

This exercise introduces the A note and places the rests on different beats of the bar. Make sure you count or tap your foot to help you play the notes at the correct time. Remember to mute the strings to ensure the rests are silent.

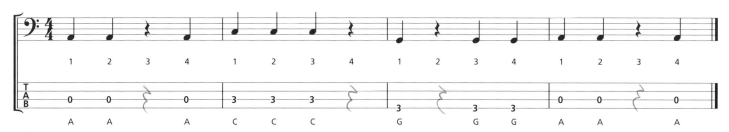

Example 4 — 'INFERNO' BARS 1-4

This example combines everything you have learned in your rock lessons and is the first four bars of the piece 'Inferno' found on page 42. Remember to count along to the pulse to help you play the notes on the correct beats.

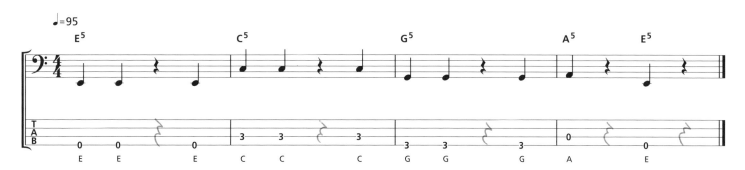

Teacher's Notes

Teacher's Rating

POP
PART 1

In this lesson you will play your first pop bassline. You'll also learn a new note and a new rhythm

DID YOU KNOW?

Larry Graham was the bassist for Sly & The Family Stone. He invented the slap bass style where the strings are slapped by the thumb rather than picked with a plectrum or fingers.

WHAT YOU WILL LEARN
☑ A new note: D
☑ Whole- and half-note rhythms

Pop music is a style of music that's all about making catchy songs that lots of people will like. One Direction, Bruno Mars and Katy Perry are some of the most famous pop acts. Most pop bands use keyboards and synthesizers to produce their sounds as well as drums, bass and guitars. Pop basslines are usually simple so they complement the song rather than stand out on their own.

RIFFS & MELODIES
Riffs are short repeated phrases that are used in lots of popular styles of music, especially rock, pop, blues and metal. Melodies are musical phrases that are longer than riffs and are usually sung by a vocalist or played by a lead instrument such as guitar or keyboard. Although bassists don't normally play a song's melody, they will sometimes play basslines that sound like melodies. These are known as melodic basslines.

Don't forget that audio is available for all the musical examples and pieces in this book. Full details on how to access the full band mixes and backing tracks can be found on page 4.

Example 1 — BASSLINE USING WHOLE NOTES & HALF NOTES

Whole notes last for four beats. Half notes last for two beats. This example uses both of these note values. Each half note should ring for two full beats, so try not to leave any gaps in between. Tap your foot or count along to the pulse to help you play the notes for the correct length.

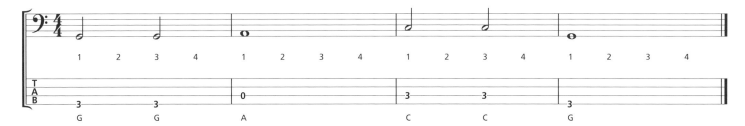

Example 2 — ADDING THE D NOTE

This exercise adds a D note, played on the open D string. Make sure you remove your finger from the C note in bar 3 to stop it ringing into the final bar.

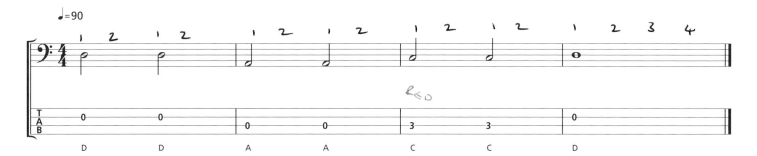

Example 3 — MIXING RHYTHMS

In this example the new half-note rhythm is combined with the quarter-note rhythm. Each bar contains a half note followed by two quarter notes. Tap your foot or count along to the pulse to play the notes in the correct place.

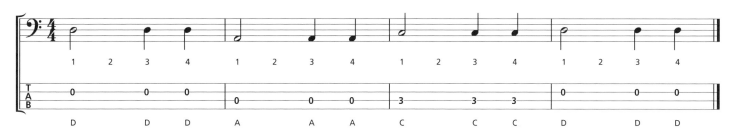

Teacher's Notes

Teacher's Rating

POP PART 2

In your second pop lesson you will be introduced to another new note and the half-note rest

Remember to rest your thumb on the string above the one you are playing

As always, keep your fingers close to, but not on top of the frets to avoid fretbuzz.

WHAT YOU WILL LEARN

☑ A new note: B
☑ Half-note rests

Your first pop lesson taught you how to play a new note and two new rhythms: whole notes and half notes. You played exercises that mixed different rhythms. In this lesson you will use these rhythms and a new rest will be introduced. By the end of this lesson you will be ready to play four bars of the piece 'Don't Stop' on page 43.

Most basses have four strings, but the five-string bass has an extra string next to the E string. It is tuned to B below E and gives a deeper sound when used. Five-string basses are especially popular in rock, metal and hip hop.

Example 1   BASSLINE USING THE B NOTE

This exercise introduces the B note and uses the rhythm of a half note and two quarter notes that was used in the last lesson. It also uses a rest in bar 1.

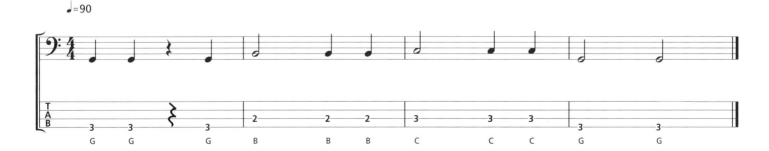

Example 2   BASSLINE USING THE HALF-NOTE REST

Half-note rests last for two beats. In this exercise a half note is played at the beginning of the bar, lasting for two beats. This is followed by a half-note rest, so the remaining two beats of the bar should be silent.

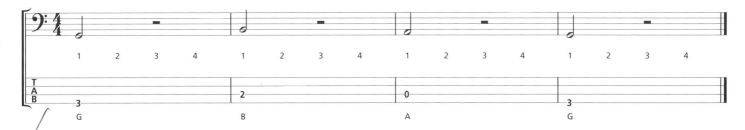

Example 3   COMBINING RHYTHMS

This example combines half-note rests with both half notes and quarter notes. Make sure your bass is completely silent during the rests by muting the strings with your picking and fretting hands.

Example 4   'DON'T STOP' BARS 13-16

This exercise will give you the chance to put everything you have learned so far into practice and is the final four bars of 'Don't Stop' found on page 43. It includes four different pitches as well as the rhythms and rests you have played in this lesson. Remember to tap your foot or count along to the pulse to help you play the notes at the right time.

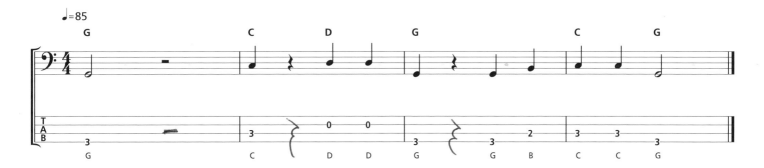

Teacher's Notes

Teacher's Rating

COUNTRY

PART 1

Your first country music lesson will introduce you to a **dotted rhythm** and a **new note**

DID YOU KNOW?

Jack Bruce was the bass player in Cream, a supergroup, with guitarist Eric Clapton and drummer Ginger Baker. Bruce mixes blues and rock influences and is very skilful.

WHAT YOU WILL LEARN
- ☑ A new note: F
- ☑ The dotted half note

Country music began in America but is now popular all over the world. Like pop music, country music is all about catchy songs, so the singer and the words are very important. Most country bands consist of drums, bass, guitar and piano. Sometimes musicians might want a more traditional sound and additional instruments such as slide guitar, mandolin, banjo, violin and harmonica are used. In this case the bass player might play a double (acoustic) bass instead of electric. In country music the bass is a supporting instrument and usually plays simple basslines made up of root notes. However, other notes from the chords can be used too. Johnny Cash, Taylor Swift and Dolly Parton are some of the most famous country acts – again, similarly to pop music, singers, not bands, are usually the stars.

A NEW NOTE & A LONGER RHYTHM

Your first country lesson will introduce you to another new note: F. You will also learn to play a new rhythm, the dotted half note.

Don't forget that audio is available for all the musical examples and pieces in this book. Full details on how to access the full band mixes and backing tracks can be found on page 4.

Example 1 — BASSLINE USING THE F NOTE

In this exercise you will play a new note: F. In bars 2 and 4 there are rests on beats two and four, so make sure there is silence during these beats by muting the strings with both your fretting and picking hands.

Example 2 — DOTTED HALF NOTES

When a dot is placed after a note, the length of the note is changed so that it lasts for its original length plus half of this value again. A dotted half note would last for three beats (two beats + one beat). This example features dotted half notes on the first beats of bars 1–4.

Example 3 — MORE DOTTED HALF NOTES

Here is another example that includes the dotted half-note rhythm. Remember to count "1 2 3 4" as you play this exercise. This will help you stay in time with the backing track.

Teacher's Notes

Teacher's Rating

COUNTRY

PART 2

Your second country lesson is an introduction to a new type of note called an octave

Using the one-finger-per-fret method will help you to play the examples in this lesson accurately.

Rest your thumb on the A string to stop it ringing out while playing the D string

WHAT YOU WILL LEARN
☑ Octaves
☑ Three new notes: high E, F and G

So far you have learned seven notes: E, F, G, A, B, C and D. The next note you will learn is another E note. This has the same sound as the E note you learned in the last lesson; however, this E sounds higher. The second E is referred to as being an octave (Latin for eighth) higher than the first because the notes are separated by eight notes of a scale. By the end of this lesson you should be ready to play the piece 'Honey Boo' on page 44.

DID YOU KNOW?

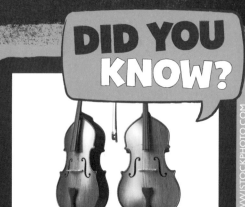

The double bass existed for years before the electric bass was invented. It was used first in orchestras, then by bass players in jazz, folk and rock 'n' roll groups. It is hollow and much larger than an electric bass.

© WWW.ISTOCKPHOTO.COM

Example 1   BASSLINE USING THE HIGH E

This example introduces an E note that's an octave higher than the E in the previous lesson. This E is played at the 2nd fret of the D string. Rest the thumb of your picking hand on the A string to stop it ringing.

♩=95

Example 2 — BASSLINE USING THE HIGH F

This exercise introduces another octave note, this time an F. This F is one octave higher than the F which is found at the 1st fret of the E string and is played at the 3rd fret of the D string. In this exercise, both new notes will be used.

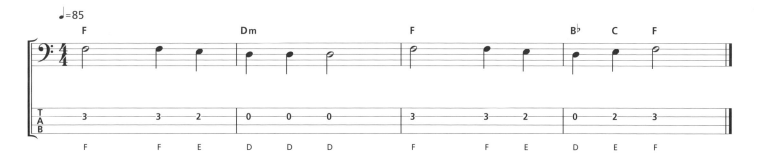

Example 3 — BASSLINE USING E, F & G

This exercise introduces a G an octave higher than the G at the 3rd fret of the E string. This note is played on the open G string. All three new octaves are used in this exercise, so start slowly without the backing track until you feel comfortable.

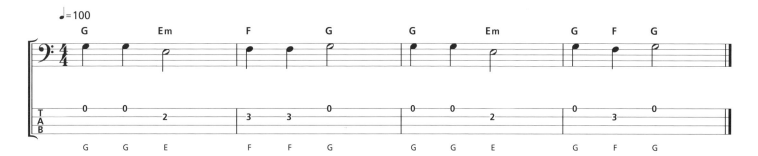

Example 4 — 'HONEY BOO' BARS 13-16

This is bars 13–16 of 'Honey Boo' on page 44. It uses dotted half notes and two of the three higher octave notes you have just learned in this lesson. The most challenging part of this melodic bassline is bars 1 and 3 where you have to skip over the D string between the first and second notes.

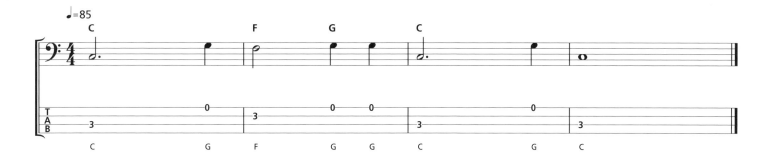

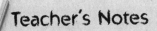

Teacher's Notes

Teacher's Rating

INDIE  PART 1

Your first indie lesson will introduce you to arpeggios and show you how to combine them with root notes

DID YOU KNOW?

The Beatles' bass player Paul McCartney is left-handed. He plays a Höfner ViolinBass, which (like a violin) has ahollowbody.It's a right-handed model upside down.

WHAT YOU WILL LEARN
☑ C major arpeggio
☑ Basslines using arpeggios

The indie style of music began in the 1980s and is mostly based on guitars. Its name is short for independent because it was released on small, *independent* record labels rather than the bigger, major labels. The Smiths, Oasis and Snow Patrol are some of the most famous indie bands. Indie basslines are often kept simple to complement the guitar and vocals, but playing simple basslines really well is more difficult than you think.

ARPEGGIOS

In your rock lesson you learned that chords are made up of two or more notes and are usually played by guitars. This lesson will teach you how chords can be played on bass, but in a different way. Guitars and keyboards will often play all the notes of a chord together. This usually doesn't sound good on bass so instead you will play each note of the chord individually in this book. This is an arpeggio.

Don't forget that audio is available for all the musical examples and pieces in this book. Full details on how to access the full band mixes and backing tracks can be found on page 4.

Example 1 — C MAJOR ARPEGGIO

This example uses the C major arpeggio. Make sure you stop pressing down at the end of each fretted note. This will stop notes from ringing into each other, which will produce a clearer sound.

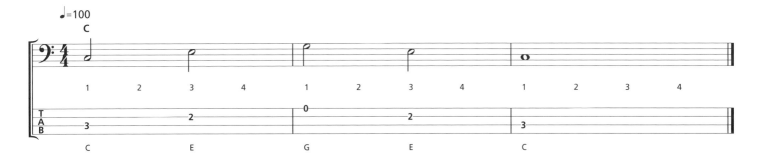

Example 2 — BASSLINE USING THE C MAJOR ARPEGGIO

This example also uses the C major arpeggio, but this time with a rhythm that combines quarter, half and whole notes. Tap your foot or count along to the pulse to make sure you play the notes on the correct beat.

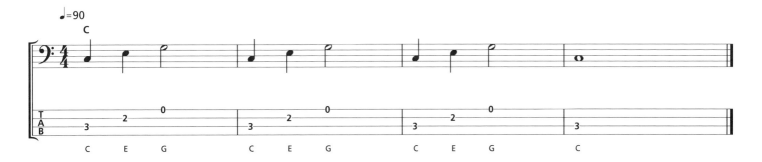

Example 3 — COMBINING AN ARPEGGIO WITH ROOT NOTES

This example uses a combination of an arpeggio and root notes. Bars 1 and 2 use the C major arpeggio, while bar 3 uses the root note of the F chord and bar 4 uses the root of the C chord.

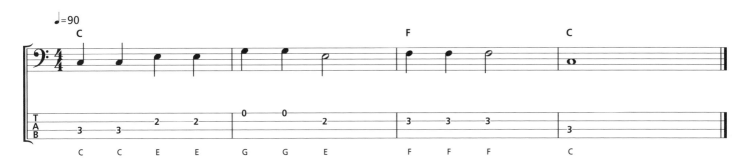

Teacher's Notes

Teacher's Rating

INDIE 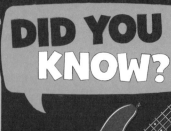 PART 2

In your second indie lesson you will be introduced to another arpeggio and the walking bassline

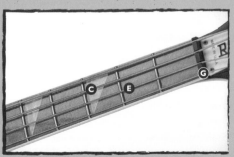

These are the notes of the C major arpeggios you learned in Indie Part 1

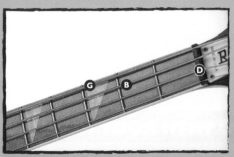

Here are the notes of the G major arpeggio you will learn in Indie Part 2

WHAT YOU WILL LEARN
☑ G major arpeggio
☑ Walking basslines

Part 2 of your indie lesson shows you a new arpeggio, G major, and introduces the walking bassline. A walking bassline is one that has a series of quarter notes played one after the other. The steady rhythm that results is a bit like the sound of feet *walking* down the street, hence the name, 'walking bassline'.

DID YOU KNOW?

Fender has designed two classic bass guitars. The Jazz Bass was introduced in 1960 with two pickups (the Precision had only one) and a slim neck that made it easier to move your hand around the fretboard. Its body was shaped for added comfort.

Example 1	BASSLINE USING G MAJOR ARPEGGIO

This example starts with each note of the arpeggio played once and then the next two bars feature each note played twice.
Avoid letting the notes ring into each other.

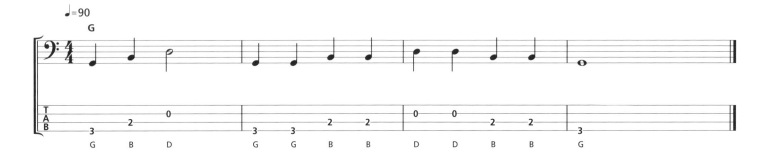

Example 2 — WALKING BASSLINE USING ARPEGGIOS

This example uses the G and C major arpeggios. Playing quarter-note arpeggios creates a part that is known as a walking bassline. All the notes in bars 1–4 should be the same length, so aim to make the example sound like a series of even notes.

Example 3 — BASSLINE COMBINING ARPEGGIOS & ROOT NOTES

Bars 1 and 3 use arpeggios, while bars 2, 4 and 5 use root notes. Play through the example and listen to the contrast between the walking arpeggios and the static, stable root notes.

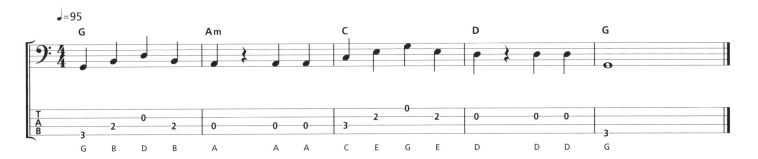

Example 4 — 'NOVA' BARS 13–16

This example puts everything you've learned in these two lessons into practice. It is bars 13–16 of the piece 'Nova', which you'll find on page 45. Make sure the notes don't ring into each other in bars 1 and 2 and that the rests in bar 3 are silent.

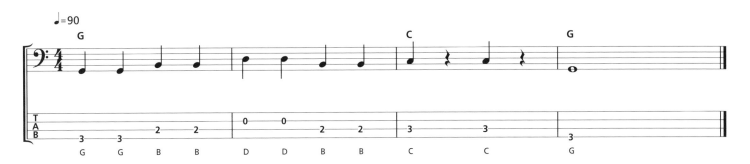

Teacher's Notes

Teacher's Rating

HIP HOP PART 1

In this introduction to hip hop you will learn all about eighth-note rhythms

DID YOU KNOW?

Bootsy Collins is a very famous funk bassist who played with James Brown and P-Funk. He is known for his star-shaped bass and star-shaped glasses. His style of bass playing is just as showy!

© TIM MOSENFELDER / CORBIS

WHAT YOU WILL LEARN
☑ Eighth-note rhythms
☑ Upstrokes and two finger technique

Most hip hop music is based on sampling. Sampling is taking a part of someone else's record and making a new piece of music with it. This was first done in the 1970s by DJs in New York who wanted to extend certain parts of the records they played

which were popular with dancers. Since then hip hop musicians have used a mixture of live instruments – including bass – and machines called samplers to produce songs that use short, catchy musical ideas that are repeated, usually for the whole of a song. Eminem, Will Smith and Jay Z are some of the most famous hip hop artists.

EIGHTH NOTES
So far you have counted the pulse as "1 2 3 4" and every note you

have played has been played at the same time as one of these numbers. If there are eighth notes in a piece you should count out "1 & 2 & 3 & 4 &".

Don't forget that audio is available for all the musical examples and pieces in this book. Full details on how to access the full band mixes and backing tracks can be found on page 4.

Example 1 BASSLINE USING EIGHT NOTES

If you are playing with a pick you should play the first eighth note in each group with a downstroke and the second with an upstroke. If you are playing with fingers, play the first eighth note with your first finger and the second with your second finger. The **N.C.** symbol lets you know that **no chord** is being played.

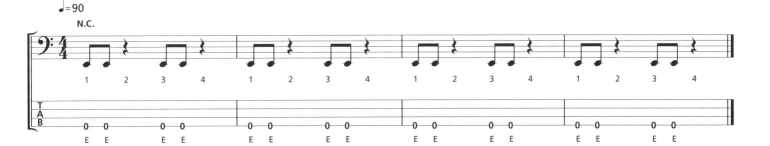

Example 2 RIFF USING EIGHTH NOTES

The eighth notes in this example follow each other quickly, so it is important that you use the first and second fingers of your picking hand (or downstrokes and upstrokes) to play this at the right speed.

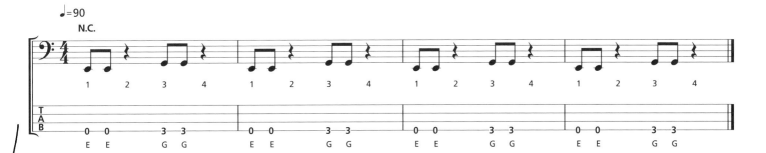

Example 3 RIFF USING A MIX OF RHYTHMS

In this exercise you will play a combination of quarter notes and eighth notes. Pay attention to the rest on beat two. As before, try to make sure that beat two is completely silent and that all the notes ring for their full length.

Tiger - shh - Pig - Pig -

Teacher's Notes

Teacher's Rating

HIP HOP PART 2

Your second hip hop lesson introduces you to a new part of written music: the key signature

An F note is played by pressing your first finger down on the 1st fret of the E string...

...while an F# is played by pressing your second finger down on the 2nd fret of the same string

WHAT YOU WILL LEARN
☑ A new note: F#
☑ Key signatures

When a sharp sign (#) is placed in front of a note, the note should be played one fret higher than usual. An F note is played on the 1st fret of the E string and an F# is played on the 2nd fret of the E string. This sharp sign is one of three musical signs known as accidentals. The other two are the flat (♭) and the natural (♮) sign.

DID YOU KNOW?

Sometimes effects are used to change the sound of the bass guitar. One of the most common effects is overdrive/distortion, which gives the bass a growling sound. This is especially popular in rock and metal.

Example 1   PLAYING F# NOTES

In this example a new note is introduced, F#, which is played at the 2nd fret of the E string. Notice that if this note is played more than once in a bar the sharp symbol is not added again because it applies to all subsequent F notes in the bar.

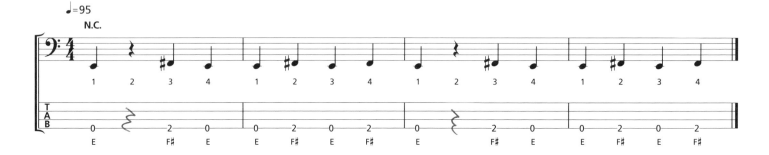

Example 2 — **USING A KEY SIGNATURE**

If a piece uses F♯ notes all the way through without any F notes (like this piece), the composer will save writing lots of F♯ notes in the music by writing a sharp symbol (♯) on the F line of the stave at the start of every line of music. This lets the bassist know that all F notes are to be played as F♯ notes. This is an example of a key signature.

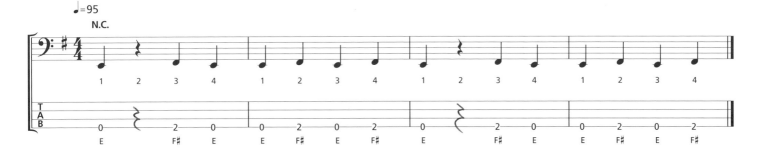

Example 3 — **RIFF USING EIGHTH NOTES**

In this example you will play a rhythm that uses quarter notes and eighth notes. Bars 2 and 4 have a rest on beat 2. These beats should be silent. Place your picking hand back on the string to stop it ringing too long.

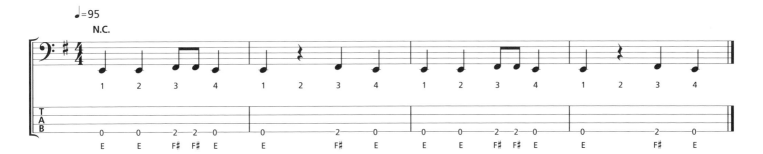

Example 4 — **'SUBSONIC' BARS 13–16**

This example shows bars 13–16 from the piece 'Subsonic' on page 46. Tap your foot to the pulse ("1 2 3 4") and count aloud in eighth notes ("1 & 2 & 3 & 4 &") to help you play the eighth notes correctly.

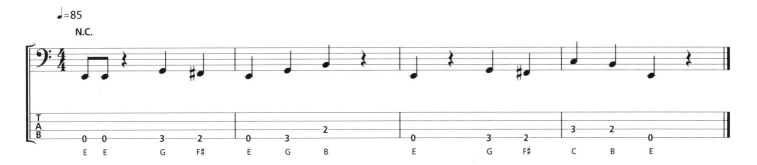

Teacher's Notes

Teacher's Rating

METAL
PART 1

Your first metal lesson shows you how to play a bassline with a pumping eighth-note rhythm

DID YOU KNOW?

Geezer Butler is the bass player for the metal group Black Sabbath. He tunes his bass down for a heavier sound and uses a wah pedal, which has inspired other metal bassists.

WHAT YOU WILL LEARN
☑ Pumping eighth-note rhythms

Metal is a style of music based on distorted guitars, which make it sound 'heavy'. The style began in the 1970s when bands started to play a more powerful version of rock than before. Bass in metal often doubles the powerful guitar riffs, but there are also lots of melodic lines to play during the quieter parts of a song.

A typical metal band consists of two guitars, vocals, drums and bass. Whether you are playing a riff or a supporting bassline, it is important to play with more force than usual to get the right sound. Black Sabbath, Metallica, Iron Maiden and Pantera are some of the most famous metal bands.

PUMPING EIGHTH-NOTE BASSLINES

Many metal songs use basslines that feature continuous eighth notes, usually played using the root notes of the chords. This provides a solid base for the other instruments to build on. Playing constant eighth notes requires stamina, though, so the examples in this lesson will feature just a few in each bar.

Don't forget that audio is available for all the musical examples and pieces in this book. Full details on how to access the full band mixes and backing tracks can be found on page 4.

Example 1 — QUARTER-NOTE BASSLINE

This example uses quarter notes on every beat and will prepare you for the next example. Make sure you strike all the notes strongly and aim to make them as even as possible.

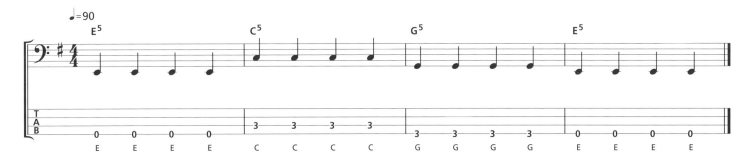

Example 2 — PUMPING BASSLINE

This example uses the same notes as Example 1, but there are eighth notes on beats 1 and 3 of every bar. Play the first eighth note with your first finger and the second with your second finger. If you are using a pick, play the first note with a downstroke and the second with an upstroke.

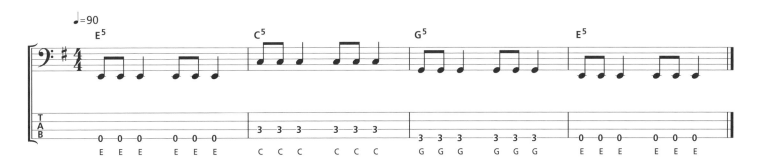

Example 3 — RIFF USING EIGHT NOTES

Here is another pumping bassline that uses eighth notes. Bar 2 alternates quarter-note fretted notes with eighth-note open strings. This is used frequently in metal. Make sure that beat four in bar 4 is silent by using your picking hand to mute the note played on beat three.

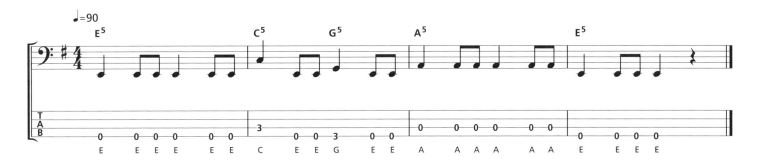

Teacher's Notes

Teacher's Rating

METAL PART 2

This second metal lesson features a final new note and shows you how to play a fill

You already know that the normal B note is played at 2nd fret of the A string...

...but the B♭ in this lesson is played at the 1st fret of the same string

WHAT YOU WILL LEARN
☑ A new note: B♭
☑ How to play a fill

So far you have learned about sharps where the sharp symbol (♯) tells you that the note to be played is one fret higher than usual. In this lesson you will learn a new note, B♭. The flat symbol (♭) means that any note next to the symbol should be played one fret lower than usual. So here, when you see B♭ in the music you should play the note one fret lower than B.

DID YOU KNOW?

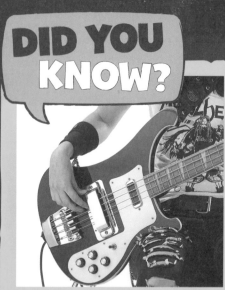

The Rickenbacker 4003 is one of the most recognisable electric basses. It has a special design where one piece of wood runs from the end of the neck to the end of the body, with two 'wings' glued either side to form the body. And it looks very cool!

Example 1   RIFF USING B♭ NOTE

This heavy riff uses a B♭ note to produce a dark sound that is common in metal. As with all metal riffs, strike the notes strongly to make the right sound for this style.

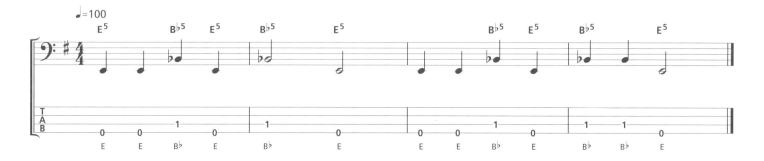

Example 2 — BASSLINE WITH FILL

This exercise starts with a quarter-note bassline, but adds a simple melodic fill in bar 4. It is quite common for bass players to add a simple fill at the end of a four-bar or eight-bar section.

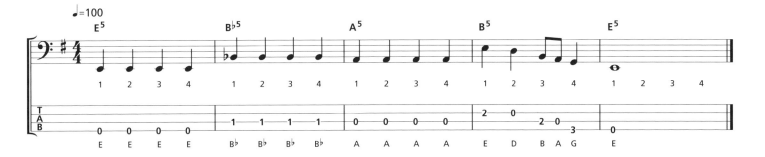

Example 3 — PUMPING BASSLINE WITH FILL

Like the previous example this bassline features a fill, but this time the bassline uses the pumping eighth-note rhythm that you played in the previous lesson. Remember to alternate between the first and second fingers of your picking hand (or down and upstrokes with a pick) on the eighth notes.

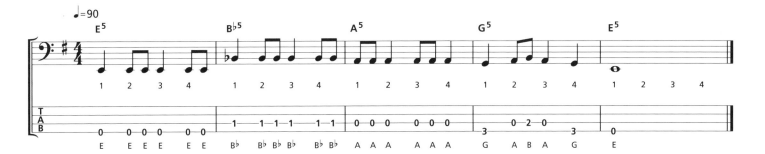

Example 4 — 'SHEET METAL' BARS 9–13

This is bars 9–13 of the piece 'Sheet Metal', which you will find on page 47. Pay close attention to the rhythms and count along to help you place the notes on the correct beat.

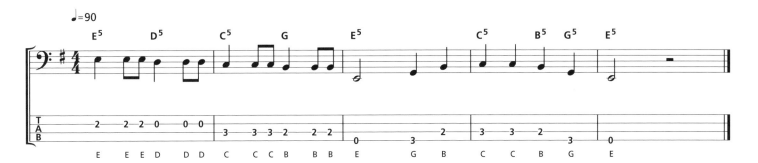

Teacher's Notes

Teacher's Rating

My Notes

PIECES
INTRODUCTION

Now that you have worked your way through the lessons and learned how to play your instrument, you are ready to perform your first full pieces of music. You will find them all in this section – one for each style of music you learned in your lessons.

There are also three extra pieces which can be played on your own or as part of a band. The other band parts can be found in *Let's Rock Guitar* and *Let's Rock Drums* and the full band score is part of your downloadable package.

ROCK
'INFERNO'

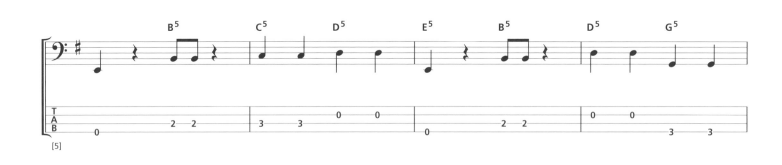

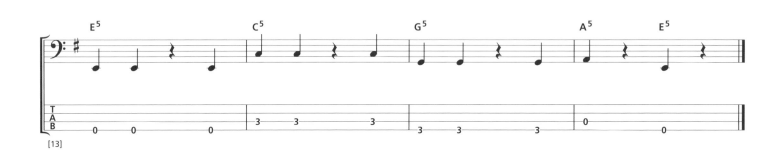

POP
'DON'T STOP'

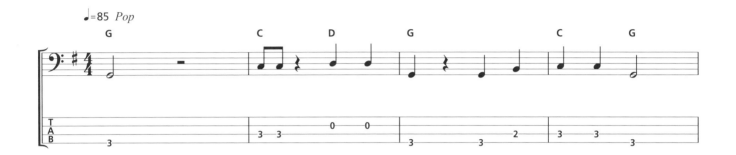

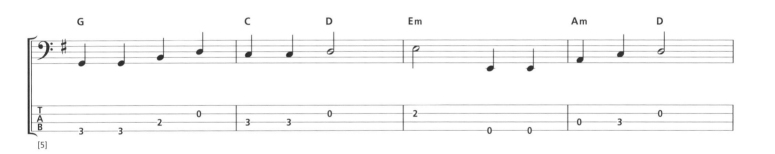

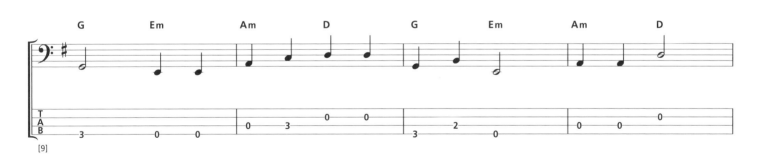

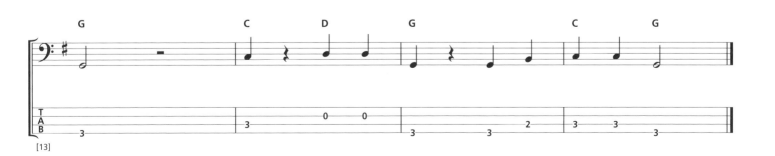

COUNTRY
'HONEY BOO'

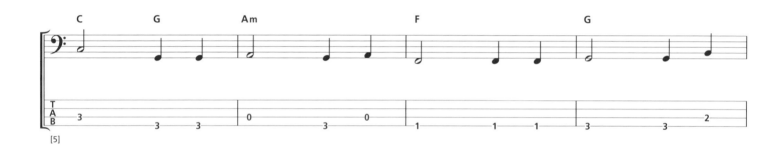

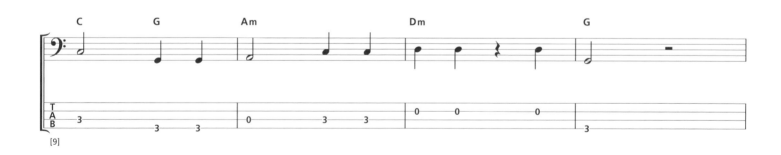

INDIE
'NOVA'

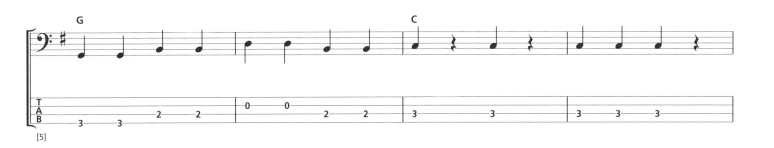

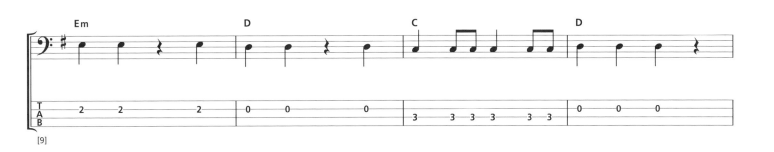

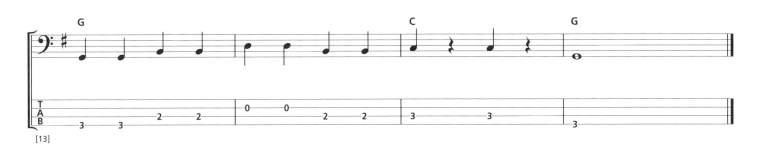

HIP HOP
'SUBSONIC'

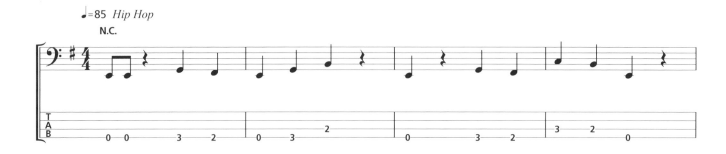

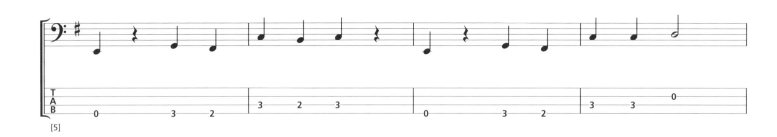

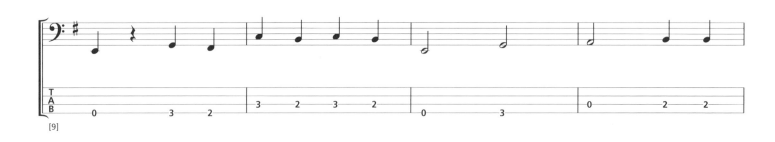

METAL
'SHEET METAL'

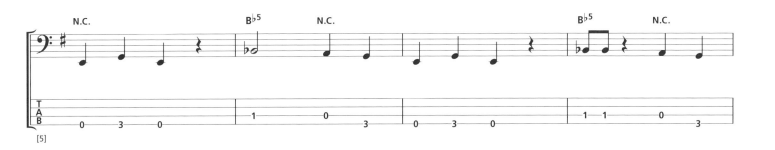

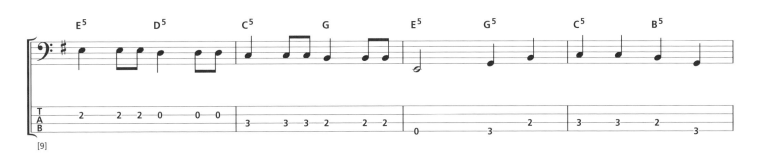

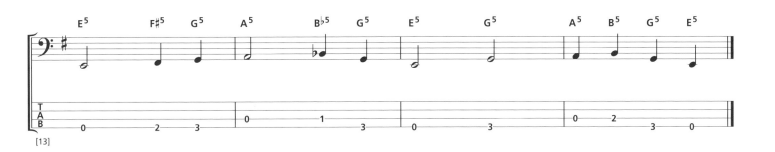

ROCK
'OVERLOAD'

PERFORMANCE PIECE!   *Practices*

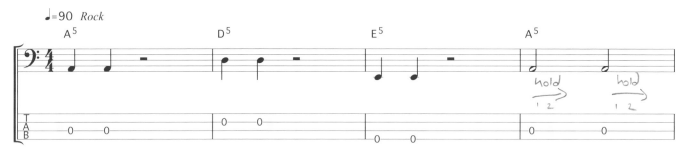

(7 notes in a row)

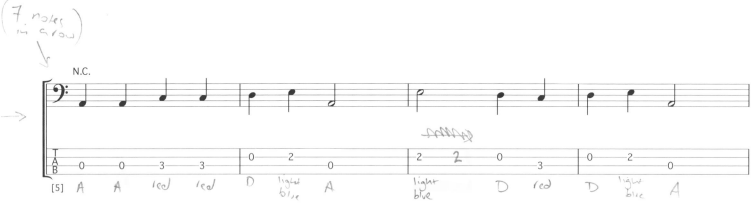

[5] A A red red D light blue A light blue D red D light blue A

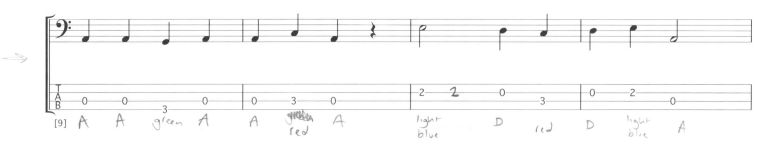

[9] A A green A A green red A light blue D red D light blue A

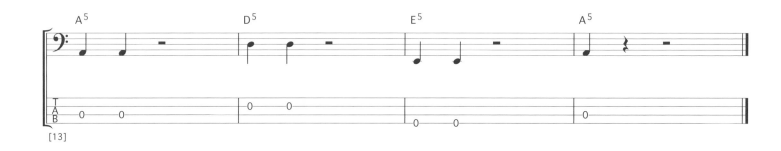

[13]

METAL
'SLAM'

28/11/17 – Practice this piece – focus on the bp line.

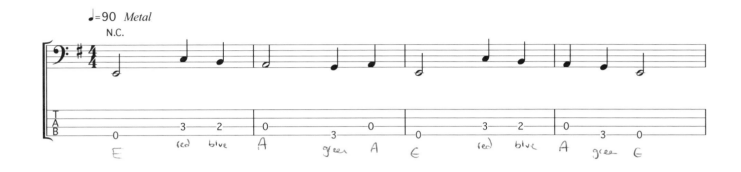

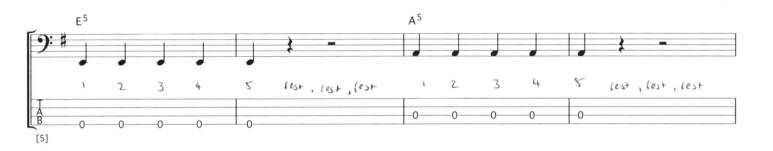

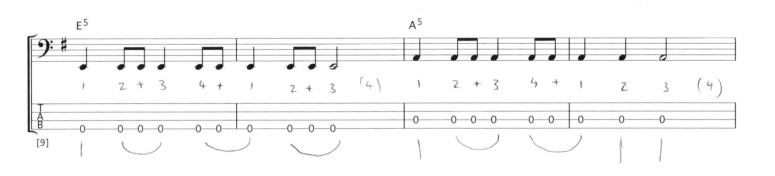

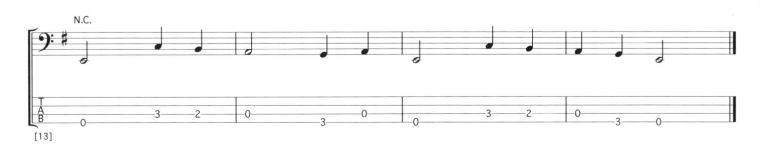

INDIE
'UNDER THE RADAR'

28/11/17 - Practice each line before trying the whole piece.

♩=90 *Indie*

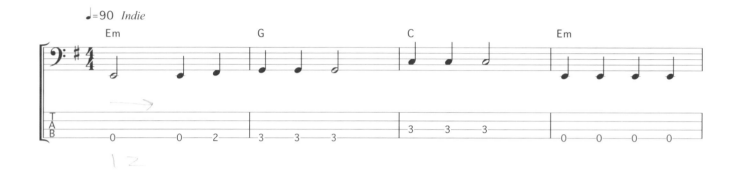

[5]

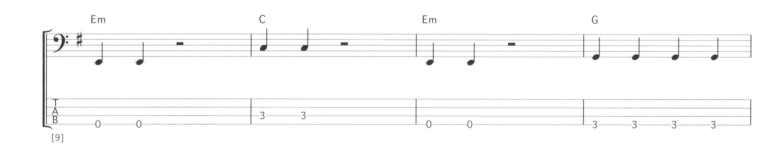

[9]

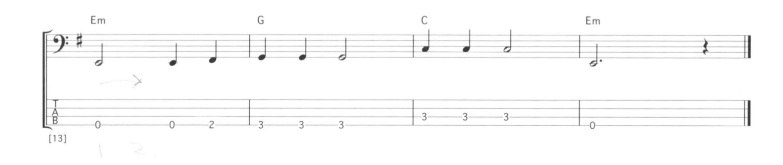

[13]

Exam Time!

THE ROCKSCHOOL PREMIERE EXAM

The pieces in this book can now be performed in an examination which is fully accredited just like every other Rockschool grade exam. There are no tests or technicals, just five performance pieces, making it the ideal introduction to Rockschool examinations. Entering a Rockschool exam is easy. You can enter online at *www.rslawards.com* or by downloading and filling in an exam entry form. The full Rockschool examination terms and conditions as well as exam periods and current fees are available from our website or by calling +44 (0)845 460 4747.

THE ROCKSCHOOL PREMIERE EXAM

ELEMENT	PASS
Performance Piece 1	12+ out of 20
Performance Piece 2	12+ out of 20
Performance Piece 3	12+ out of 20
Performance Piece 4	12+ out of 20
Performance Piece 5	12+ out of 20
TOTAL MARKS	60%+